Startup Stories

Founder Experiences Building Tech Companies for All While Elevating Diverse Communities

First Edition

Christopher C. King, M.P.A., M.B.A.

SAN DIEGO

Bassim Hamadeh, CEO and Publisher
Peaches diPierro, Acquisitions Editor
Danielle Gradisher, Senior Project Editor
Rachel Kahn, Production Editor
Jess Estrella, Senior Graphic Designer
Alexa Lucido, Licensing Manager
Natalie Piccotti, Director of Marketing
Kassie Graves, Senior Vice President, Editorial

Printed in the United States of America.

CONTENTS

SPECIAL THANKS

To the founders that shared their stories, I am immensely grateful for the candor and clarity of your vision to solve enduring problems of our time. Thank you for your work and conviction and resolve to see through all of your victories, both small and grand.

INTRODUCTION

These cases were selected to introduce you to a diverse group of companies and sectors, many of which you should be familiar with as a consumer. If not, see this as an opportunity to do some high-level research to familiarize yourself with where each company was founded, when and how they began engaging their customers, and some historical benchmarks of the company's development.

As you read through the cases, I encourage you to review them slowly. Take notes on important happenings, as defined by journalists, and spot potential issues that pique your curiosity while reading. In your first reading of the case, look for moments that stand out to you right away and that you may have initial questions about. In your second reading of the case, dive into moments you may have missed. Jot down some notes in the margin if you have the paper copy. If you have a digital copy, create a separate notes document, and start with important moments. Use your judgment to develop these, and then push toward what issues you see in the cases and risks for the decision maker around those high-stakes moments, and then begin to chart a path for your executive recommendation for the firm.

While you progress in reading cases throughout this text, I'd like you to develop the skill of identifying risks of each recommendation and some contingency plans for your recommended strategies. Be patient with yourself as you develop this skill; we will work on it together over time. Lastly, enjoy the cases included and put yourself in the seat of the leaders of these teams. They were deliberately selected to challenge you and to advance your critical thinking in real world situations.

1

Goodfynd

Solving the Problem of Finding Your Favorite Food During a Pandemic

Introduction

By reading this case, you will dive deeper into an industry that has widespread impact during the COVID pandemic. How we get our food and what the consumer is willing to do to get food in nutritional deserts fueled this entrepreneur. Your learning starts with examining the problem the entrepreneur and founding team targeted as well as examining the market opportunity. You will analyze the market size and the impact of the solution in the United States and then think through the ways this team of innovators can execute and what barriers they may face during execution. Finally, you will ask yourself how the team might attract investment and the counterarguments they may encounter during fundraising.

Learning Outcomes

- Identify a market opportunity with a general understanding of team building to begin shaping a solution.
- Begin analyzing market problems with a starting point of how to quantify pain points for stakeholders (e.g., how many food trucks have pain points that connect to the solution from this company).

Key Terms Used in This Chapter

- **disruption:** when a market entrant disturbs an existing market with a product or service that fundamentally changes how consumers perceive that industry. For example, YouTube changed how consumers watch videos online.
- **in-store experience:** consumers' end-to-end experience in a store
- **marketplace:** a place where selling and purchasing occurs. This could be online or offline.
- **point of sale:** where and when a consumer purchases an item
- **primary market:** the initial target market for a product or service. This includes a diverse range of granularity with psychographic and demographic characteristics. For example, a target market could include age, geographic location, buying habits, typical activities, purchasing power of household, median income, discretionary spending monthly and/or annually, hobbies, likes and dislikes, aesthetic preferences, daily style choices, discount preferences, and so on.

Section I: Business Description

Goodfynd simplifies the booking of mobile food services. The company was founded in 2018. The company has been thriving in the pandemic, capitalizing on the disruption of the financial technology services industry. The company's solution combines a point-of-sale experience with both community and search functions for more diverse food options. The founder characterizes the spirit of food trucks today as an opportunity for people from all different backgrounds who love to make delicious food to get involved in a growing marketplace. With a decrease in staffing and an unprecedented shuttering of restaurants, the mobile food industry has surged. Patrons have skipped the in-store experience and consistently ordered through apps in the past several years. Data shows that by March of 2020, this amounted to a 20% decrease in revenue for 48,000 restaurants and 4,600 bars (Dishman, n.d.).

Section II: Founder History

Goodfynd's founders are Sofiat Abdulrazaaq, Kyle Miller, and Lemaire Stewart. The three met during their undergraduate studies at Virginia Tech. Abdulrazaaq studied political science and psychology, Miller studied apparel housing and resource management, and Stewart studied electrical and computer engineering. Abdulrazaaq later worked at several nonprofits and fortune 500 companies in product development and innovation. She studied law at American University and earned a masters in Global Affairs from the University of Denver. Miller was previously in property management before attending an immersive UX training program. Stewart is a software engineer, having received his bachelor's from Virginia Tech and his master's from George Mason University.

Concept Highlight

user experience (UX) design: the layered interfaces that the user (aka the customer) touches and actively manipulates to produce a desired result. While the UX is occurring, the software typically captures and measures this experience, allowing for the back-end technology to produce reports on the effectiveness or lack of effectiveness of the design.

Section III: Company History

Concept Highlight

business model: a term of art describing how a business plans to make money

The company was founded in 2018, aiming to make locally made food accessible, while enabling small and growing food businesses to better serve their customers (Graham, 2020). Their business model leverages the existing purchasing power of takeout orders by charging a fee for service on existing orders. Preorders can also be made on the platform, while truck owners can set schedules, manage and accept those preorders, and sign up for events in partnership with properties looking to cater or provide food truck options to larger crowds.

The additional features evolved after market research and proof of concept in the District of Columbia, Maryland, and Virginia area. The company exceeded $100k in revenue in 2020 after participating in the SeedSpot DC Impact Accelerator and LightHouse Labs programs. By 2019, Goodfynd operated 400 food trucks in Richmond, Washington DC, and parts of Maryland. The company is dedicated to small business growth and has learned to move to targeting high traffic areas. The company focuses on contactless payments and is committed to supporting minority-led enterprises; in their primary markets, 80% of food truck owners are non-White (Goodfynd, n.d.). They then evolved to partnering with residential buildings and supporting outside events to attract customers.

Section IV: Current Challenges

Goodfynd is venture backed and raising investor funding. Sofiat Abdulrazaaq shared that their goal is to increase investor interest to go beyond their $1.8M raise during their first round of funding. They are interested in new geographic areas to increase revenue and sustain their momentum.

When asked about Goodfynd's current challenges, she shared the following:

> We are doing something that hasn't been done before. You see a lot of innovation in vertical spaces, building technology for a specific industry within an industry. Building a product is what we do well. There is a lot of innovation in smaller sectors that are ripe for invention. Some of the best startups in the world benefit from having a scalability playbook already. The scalability road map doesn't exist clearly.

Concept Highlight

dual-sided marketplace: a platform for economic exchange between two distinct user groups that provide each other the benefits of a large network for trade (Two-Sided Marketplace, n.d.).

Learning the customers can be very dynamic in the dual-sided marketplace. This would be characterized as both B2B and B2C. Some of the decisions involved here are processing information from these customers to create a business advantage. This can be tough for us as we are looking to go further faster, which may create blind spots with new people and innovation options at our disposal. There are times when I willfully do not address issues and information as it comes in.

Traditional business challenges include team performance, hiring, and expansion. From an operational standpoint, team building includes evaluating performance, supporting various levels of team members, hiring slowly, while simultaneously managing the speed of the company's growth. I believe in fire fast and hire slow. For further insight, Lemaire and Sofiat are running the company after its founding. There is a product team, sales team and associated members, marketing team and associated team, and operations. Abdul went on to describe the challenges as "identifying a role and filling it is the easy part, but operationalizing it and building out the work is the hard part."

Section V: Current Opportunities

When asked about Goodfynd's current opportunities, Sofiat Abdulrazaaq had this to say:

> As a leader, I'm always focused on what gets my company to the next level. Finding it is step one and building it is step two, the execution part. We have to wow our customers in the exact way they want to be wowed. How do I make the best decisions to execute on a product?
>
> As a woman founder and leader who is usually considered likeable, leveraging that and the network effect of being able to enhance investor confidence to raise more money. The opportunity here is to be comfortable saying "I don't know" in spaces where the founding team are pinned down on the "why me" question. Knowing that being yourself can garner millions of dollars can also be an exceptional asset.
>
> Continuing to go deeper into the customer experience on the B2B and B2C sides. The deeper we go, the more pain points we uncover. One of our pillars is simplicity to super complex problems with clear and simple solutions. To make products and features that are very intuitive. For example, we learned that there a lot of tech is native

to Gen Z, but we wanted to make something that engaged baby boomers intuitively through button placement and sizing.

Concept Highlight

B2B: business to business sales—a business model term intended to characterize to whom the business is selling
B2C: business to consumer sales—a business model term intended to characterize to whom the business is selling

Company News

Read the following news on Goodfynd to gather insight on the founder's vision and leadership team:

- Ep. 58—Sofiat Abdulrazaaq, CEO/Co-Founder, Goodfynd—*Atlanta Startup Podcast*: https://atlantastartuppodcast.com/sofiat-abdulrazaaq-ceo-co-founder-goodfynd/

Concept Highlight

fintech: "financial technology," designed to reduce friction in the buying process. For existing behavior, where the consumer is already known to engage in a transaction, the software deployed captures a fee for service while improving the experience of the customer.

Key Takeaways

- Customer experience largely dictates the fintech journey. Gaps in customer data are part of the product development process. Finding those gaps and pursuing deeper data insights must be done to reduce friction for customers.
- Underestimated founders can be very appealing to investors looking for scrappy and innovative leaders working on solutions in emerging markets.

- Team mistakes can be highly detrimental to growing ventures. "Fire fast and hire slow" as a mantra is extremely critical to the success of the venture and investor relations discussions.

Resources

- Goodfynd—Valor Venture: https://valor.vc/company/goodfynd/
- Goodfynd—Crunchbase Company Profile and Funding: https://www.crunchbase.com/organization/goodfynd
- Goodfynd Google Play App: Goodfynd: Point of Sale (POS)—Apps on Google Play
- Food Truck Platform Goodfynd Just Hit $100K in Revenue. Here's How it Plans to Keep Growing—Technical.ly: https://technical.ly/startups/food-truck-platform-goodfynd-100k-revenue-plans-growing-covid19/
- Goodfynd—Alignable: https://www.alignable.com/fairfax-va/goodfynd
- Goodfynd Events: https://events.goodfynd.com/register
- Goodfynd's Food Truck Platform Continues Fast Growth, Reaches $100K in Revenue—Richmond Inno (The Business Journals): https://www.bizjournals.com/richmond/inno/stories/profiles/2020/08/07/saas-platform-goodfynd-reaches-100k-in-revenue.html
- Kabob Mix—Goodfynd: https://events.goodfynd.com/register
- About Us—The Artemis Fund: https://www.theartemisfund.com/about-us

References

Dishman, L. (n.d.). *The delivery app landscape is changing and sustaining businesses during COVID-19*. CO—by U.S. Chamber of Commerce. https://www.uschamber.com/co/good-company/launch-pad/coronavirus-pandemic-food-delivery-businesses

Goodfynd. (n.d.). Valure Ventures. https://valor.vc/company/goodfynd/

Graham, M. (2020, July 17). *$100K in revenue. Here's how it plans to keep growing.* Technical.ly. https://technical.ly/2020/07/17/food-truck-platform-goodfynd-100k-revenue-plans-growing-covid19/

Two-Sided Marketplace. (n.d.). Reason Street. https://reasonstreet.co/business-model-two-sided-marketplace/

2

Future Capital

The Mindset Shift Problem When Creating a New Consumer Behavior

"I believe the root of this revolving door of lookalike founders is the insular nature of the venture capital community. Investors are inherently motivated, financially and socially, to close deals with members in their immediate networks. This is based on conscious and unconscious biases that create significant disadvantages to large swaths of the business community. Whether they're intended, these biases create barriers to entry that disproportionately affect minority founders."

—Marlon Thompson, CEO and founder of Marlon Capital

Introduction

By reading this case study, you will learn about startup challenges you may not have been exposed to until now. The company discussed in this chapter was developed with a significant hurdle to overcome: a knowledge gap within its customer base. Currently, information about startup investing is available from a very complex series of resources.

The available platforms provide data driven information that can be hard to receive and apply to real-world examples. Future Capital was created to provide educational resources and democratize access to angel investing, marking a sharp difference in the field. This innovation is designed to engage a diverse group of future investors, which may then affect ownership at scale.

Learning Outcomes

- Understand how funds are raised for startup leaders with technology solutions.
- Gain familiarity with investment theses, defining the thesis, the tailored principles and ethos that inform the thesis, and inferring validation of the thesis.
- Learn about removing the veil on startup investment education as well as what motivates an investor and the company.

Key Terms Used in This Chapter

- **derisk:** minimizing the risk of running a business or investing in a business
- **pre-money:** a term used to describe the valuation of a company before any rounds of financing that gives investors a picture of what the company's current value may be (Kenton, 2022)
- **startup investment:** investing in a company's growth in exchange for equity. Startup investing is widely considered one of the riskiest investment types, due to the lack of financial history of the firm. The founder's personal and business history is usually scrutinized when pursuing investment. Pedigree via academic history or big brand employers and success in high-stakes environments are often notable for early stage investments.
- **underrepresented:** in this context, defined by representation through a narrow channel of funding. "Underrepresented" refers to Black people, indigenous people, or people of color, who receive under 1% of venture capital investments (Ross & Lounibos, 2022).

Section I: Business Description

The company is working on creating a more diverse group of startup investors at different levels (angel, syndicate, and LP). They provide a learning and networking environment that allows emerging investors to have a significant impact with minimal involvement. Their approach to startup investing is unique and aims to empower underrepresented investors by providing them with education and opportunities. Additionally, they collaborate with members of their network to address the main challenge in the industry, which is access to deal flow.

Section II: Founder History

The founder of Future Capital, Marlon Thompson, explains his journey to founding the company as follows: he grew up in Scarborough, a suburb of Toronto, in a lower middle-class household raised by a single parent. Despite studying public administration and political science in university, he ended up working as an operations manager in the apparel industry for large retailers. After spending 9 years in the tech industry, he developed a desire to delve deeper into decision-making in venture capital. He felt that people with unconventional backgrounds like his were often excluded from positions of power. He then became a director, helping raise funds and connecting founders to the community. He also played a role in finding limited partners (LPs) and assisting partners in raising a $20 million fund, which focused on larger enterprise de-risk investments. The emphasis of their technology was on corporate relationships..

Concept Highlight

fund development: the essential partner of fundraising. It is accomplished through the process of relationship building, nurturing loyalty, and lifetime value for every investor or funder (philanthropy). Fundraising is often measured by initial investment and commensurate follow on investment.

Section III: Company History

Future Capital was founded to address the problem of a lack of founder diversity in tech companies. The lack of founder diversity in startup technology also contributes to this funding gap. Thompson points to a study by First Round (10 Years First Round, n.d.) that illuminates Silicon

Valley's influence: The "halo" effect with founders who have worked for Google, Apple, Facebook, Microsoft, or Amazon will lead to more likely landing "pre-money valuations 50% higher than their peers." In addition, where you go to school matters; the Ivies, Stanford, MIT, Caltech. However, as Thompson points out, for Black students or women, none of these universities fall within the top 5 engineering schools.

The funding gap is rooted in history. Brookings Institute (McIntosh et al., 2020) uncovered the net worth of White American families to be 10 times that of Black families, who originated from historic discrimination emanating from the nation's 200+ years of slavery through to Jim Crow laws and the establishment of Black Codes that further disenfranchised the Black population and enforced racial segregation in the Southern United States for over a century. Further, this gap is rooted in a history of geographical redlining, where minority communities with historically higher mortgage defaults experienced disproportionate access to government services and basic access to housing, employment, and credit. Because of the historical oppression, it is less likely a Black founder will have the initial capital to invest through family wealth.

Thompson contends that this unfair advantage sets the stage for perpetuation of practices based on a default to what's familiar. Track records continue to play a significant role in startup success. Because early-stage companies do not have history to help build investor confidence, investors will likely bet on repeat founders and investor referrals, even though the data indicates repeat founders don't necessarily perform better. Thompson explains,

> I founded Future Capital when I was still working at the venture firm. August 2020, felt like the right time shortly after the death of George Floyd. There initially was an angel investment crash course that tested our concept. This has iterated to be built by outsiders for outsiders.
>
> Key hires and the thinking behind building the team started with the founder in lockdown at the beginning of COVID. A technical advisor joined to help with the early roadmap. The first actual hire was a development expert at 6 months. The second hire was a marketing specialist for the first year. The technical advisor scoped out the build of the platform about a year in. We made some mistakes by bringing in a salesperson in the first year and that was a major learning experience for me. We learned that quality over quantity was super important here. The first phase of validation and customer

discovery and development elevated that there was no one size fits all for us.

Section IV: Current Challenges

Concept Highlight

angel investor: someone who provides financial backing for small startups or entrepreneurs. Typically, this backing is in exchange for ownership equity in the company. The funds angel investors provide may be a one-time investment to help the business get off the ground or an ongoing injection to support and carry the company through difficult early stages.

The current challenges (as of spring of 2023) of the business include validating and garnering mainstream support for angel investor education and raising capital to fuel the company's growth. Thompson is also recruiting advisors who serve the C-suite to advance the company's relationship capital:

> I wish we could move faster.
>
> The first 8 months we validated core questions around who our current customers are and what they want to do. How we can help them do it. We just need more people now and more resources.
>
> My job as a founder has shifted from creation to stakeholder development, and relationship management. Energetically it feels different. I'm enjoying the stakeholder management, but it is more draining. Refilling my cup is a work in progress, including time with loved ones. Keeping the quality of my relationships high is helpful.

Company News

Read the following news on Future Capital for insight into the founder's vision and the problems trending in venture capital that the team is focusing on:

- "Future Capital Enables a Diverse Cohort of Investors to Close the Funding Gap"—Forbes: https://www.forbes.com/sites/hessiejones/2020/12/10/future-capital-enables-a-diverse-cohort-of-investor-to-close-the-funding-gap/

Key Takeaways

This case features a novel approach to solving the problem of closing generational wealth gaps. While the company engages in education, it also creates an opportunity for direct startup investment analysis and investments. The owner (as a shareholder) is now the underrepresented individual. This approach puts the community first but also provides a fintech experience that was otherwise limited to those wealthy individuals in the room at the time of the raise.

Resources

- Future Capital Enables a Diverse Cohort of Investor to Close the Funding Gap—PSIAI: https://psiai.com/?p=1033
- Meet the man changing the face of startup funding—Vancouver Tech Journal: https://www.vantechjournal.com/p/future-capital-marlon-thompson?s=r
- Not Your Grandfather's Equity Investing—Vancouver Tech Journal: https://www.vantechjournal.com/p/tech-briefing-marlon-thompson?s=r
- First Round 10 Year Project: https://10years.firstround.com/
- The Future of Capital: Women—Squarespace: https://static1.squarespace.com/static/5fa9ce6eae5ca53a8002e02a/t/5fc6f396a-d3e64119238cecf/1606874014155/The+Future+of+Capital_+Women.pdf
- Bridging the Black Founders Venture Capital Gap—Accenture: https://www.accenture.com/us-en/insights/technology/black-founders#:~:text=In%20brief%201%20Black%20founders%20are%20at%20an,in%20business%20opportunities%20are%20being%20lost.%20More%20items

- Pre-Money Valuation Definition—Investopedia: https://www.investopedia.com/terms/p/premoneyvaluation.asp#:~:text=Pre-money%20is%20the%20valuation%20of%20a%20company%20before,of%20financing%2C%20whether%20that%27s%20private%20or%20public%20investment

References

10 Year First Round Project. (n.d.). https://10years.firstround.com/

Kenton, W. (2022, April 26). *Pre-money valuation: Overview, types and examples.* Investopedia. https://www.investopedia.com/terms/p/premoneyvaluation.asp#:~:text=Pre-money%20is%20the%20valuation%20of%20a%20company%20before,of%20financing%2C%20whether%20that%27s%20private%20or%20public%20investment.

McIntosh, K., Moss, E., Nunn, R., & Shambaugh, J. (2020). *Examining the Black-White wealth gap.* Brookings Institute. https://www.brookings.edu/articles/examining-the-black-white-wealth-gap/

Ross, K., & Lounibos, T. (2022, February 16). *Bridging the Black founders venture capital gap.* Accenture. https://www.accenture.com/us-en/insights/technology/black-founders#:~:text=In%20brief%201%20Black%20founders%20are%20at%20an,in%20business%20opportunities%20are%20being%20lost.%20More%20items

3

Henry Health

The Problem of Proving an Initial Concept and Expansion: Henry Health Rebranded to Hurdle

"You can find investors and become part of a network that cements and reaffirms your values."

"Founders should eventually become CEOs, but not all founders can make the transition to CEO."

"Those of us who have a business that has social impact value don't get to escape the responsibility of making money for our investors."

—Kevin Dedner

Concept Highlight

regulatory landscape: a series of laws that affect the staffing and go-to market strategy
execution at scale: key performance indicators accomplished
social impact venture and venture capital (VC) tensions: VC investors typically care most about the return on their investment and the scale of the solution. They tend to care less about the social impact, which creates a tension point for founders pursuing capital.
team-growth fit: often an extension of the leadership team's business acumen. This fit is essential to navigate as the team expands and the roles either narrow or fundamentally shift; founding staff may not always be fit to grow with the founding staff may not always be fit to grow with the firm.

Introduction

Hurdle built a business through identifying the growing mental health challenges faced by diverse communities and crafted a service model with their technology to reduce barriers of access to culturally intentional teletherapy. The company was founded on the inspiring story of the founder, which led to a desire to extend the life expectancy of Black men through mental health services. His personal mission led to a significant investment in product development, team, culture, and the company's initial growth strategy. During his initial raise, he was underestimated and regularly told he was uninvestable. While reading this case, take note of how you think the founding team developed their initial goals and their clarity on the data that led to their innovative solution. Bridge this thinking, and then develop your own hypotheses of why they expanded their target market and what you believe they might do to serve more customers.

Learning Outcomes

- Understand what a moonshot goal is for a company, while connecting this concept to the mission of the venture.
- Map how the business plans to achieve a moonshot goal and subgoals.
- Understand target segments, pivots, and how an organizational chart may change over time, given the evolution of an early-stage venture to their Series-A level.
- The desired outcome is for students to synthesize case issues and learn how to recommend additional growth goals for the firm.

Key Terms Used in This Chapter

- **capital:** anything that confers value or benefit to its owner such as financing, financial assets, machinery, or intellectual property (Hargrave, 2022)

- **moonshot goal:** originates from the "moonshot" speech, when President John F. Kennedy challenged U.S. citizens to shoot for the moon during the space race (September 12, 1962).
- **stigma:** a mark of shame or discredit (Dictionary.com, n.d.)
- **synthesize:** combining several things into a coherent whole (Merriam-Webster, n.d.). This is the process of breaking down and creating a story for yourself, while highlighting areas of interest for you. Take copious notes to unpack the case and think beyond your personal perspective into the people mentioned in the case.
- **systemic racism:** discrimination or unequal treatment on the basis of membership in a particular ethnic group, arising from systems, structures, or expectations that have become established within society or an institution (Cambridge Dictionary, n.d.). These policies and practices exist throughout a whole society or organization and result in and support a continued unfair advantage to some people based on race.
- **target market:** a group of people with some shared characteristics that a company has identified as potential customers for its products (Investopedia Team, 2023)

Section I: Business Description

Hurdle is a mental health teletherapy solution for culturally intentional care. The company began as Henry Health in 2018, founded by Kevin Dedner. The focus at the time was to provide mental health teletherapy services specifically for Black men (Coward, 2021). The goal then was to design a product that would address the relatively low life expectancy of Black men in the United States. According to Bond and Herman (2016) this number is 72.2 years old. The founder cites the causes as complex, yet directly connected to systemic and systematic racism for which healthcare in the United States fails to address adequately at scale (Hurdle Health, n.d.). To break the stigma of mental health care, Dedner set out to create a mental health movement that destigmatizes therapy by staffing psychiatrists that specialize in and who have a clear understanding of the effects of being Black in the United States.

Section II: Founder History

Kevin is originally from Arkansas, where he began his founder journey. Dedner moved to Washington, DC, in 2011, with a public health consulting practice. Back then, he had no idea he'd venture into the work he's doing now as a tech founder. Dedner recalls "while growing my consulting practice, I worked myself into mental exhaustion that led to a period of depression."

After this period of darkness, Dedner started exploring a career in digital health, which led to the birth of Hurdle. Dedner founded the company in 2017 as Henry Health, which has since rebranded to Hurdle. The company's business model is focused on selling its platform directly to employers, as opposed to consumers, which Dedner is hoping will help scale Hurdle in the long run.

"One of the things about our business right now is that we're also in the process of learning the business as we go. We may have a couple of deficits as we understand how to scale this business much faster," Dedner said. "It's been a slow process to figure out how to build the business, but I think we've got a nice blueprint shaping up now on how to move the business forward."

The company started providing therapy in 2019 but has seen a larger demand for its services since the pandemic hit last year and more people became open to the concept of telehealth. He said mental health issues, like he experienced, are common within the Black community, and he wants to remove the stigma of seeking out therapy.

"Unfortunately, 50% of African Americans terminate therapy prematurely because of provider fit," he said. "If the thesis of our company is true, we'll change that."

Like most Black tech founders, Dedner has struggled to raise venture capital. Despite closing a seed round, he's still thinking of ways to finance his company over the long run and hopes the investment community will start devoting more time to taking pitches from minority founders: "The thing about raising venture capital is that it is incredibly hard," Dedner said. "I think it's inherently unfair to people from disadvantaged backgrounds."

The company, which also closed a small friends and family round at the beginning of 2020, has raised nearly $6 million, all told. With the fresh seed funding, Dedner is hoping to add some key hires to Hurdle's team of nine by the end of March 2021.

"Human nature is to get comfortable, they continuously try to find a way to make it comfortable working here. It's in our DNA to try to get comfort. I want people to be burning with an understanding that everything is still in flux, and nothing is promised here yet."

Section III: Company History

The company started in 2018, inspired by the founder's experience with mental health services after a period of depression. The original name of the firm was Henry Health, designed to specifically engage Black men in teletherapy. According to O'Malley (2021), only 2% of the estimated 41,000 psychiatrists in the United States are Black, and just 4% of psychologists are Black, leading to an extreme gap in culturally competent care. Henry Health's founding team believed this lack of culturally intentional care contributes directly to the life expectancy of Black men.

As the company raised venture capital, it broadened its initial targeted market, while still serving Black men directly. They also expanded their obtainable market to engage diverse families, inclusive of gender, sexuality, and racial differences, while pursuing thought leadership campaigns explaining why barriers to mental health services exist. Recently, they hosted a panel discussion on Capitol Hill convening expert clinicians to bring to light data on the experiences of diverse populations.

Since raising over $5 million from investors, the company has achieved annual revenue of $1 million+ at an $8 million+ valuation. They continue to serve their desired community of diverse families and reduce barriers to teletherapy. Their partnerships include Cigna Healthcare, Oscar Health, and Hopelab, to name a few (Lindsay, 2022).

Section IV: Current Challenges

The company was challenged with a reduction in staff, due to the summer 2022 recession forecasts. The venture capital raised has put pressure on the business for revenue growth and has made strong appeals to big brand customers (e.g., large health care companies and retailers). The company also has regular talent and culture shaping needs that startups who hire aggressively often must embrace.

Storming, norming, and forming is the best way to think about this at a growing startup. "Storming" here means attacking challenges in an all-hands-on-deck fashion. "Norming" refers to when team members get adjusted to the rhythm of work streams and cultural norms of the day-to-day interactions during meetings. Senior-level teams tend to do this well, with fewer challenges than junior-level teams, who are getting accustomed to current work norms. "Forming" is when the structure of the organization creates efficiencies in communication and deliverables on time and up to industry standards. This is handled most clearly when hiring is mapped by the needs of the organization and the last two phases are managed with minimal turnover.

Company News

Read the following news on Hurdle to hear directly from the founder about his vision and experience leading his venture:

- "StartUp Health TV 2020: Kevin Dedner, MPH, & Jeff Johnson, Hurdle"—StartUp Health: https://youtu.be/xSpjg-kv83Q
- "At Hurdle, Kevin Dedner Is Building 'Cultural Responsiveness' Into Mental Health Services": https://youtu.be/w4v45CpmS18

Key Takeaways

- Hurdle shifted to Henry Health to serve a broader audience and reach more customers.
- As Hurdle's target market expanded, they achieved more traction and attracted more investment.
- The development of strategic partnerships fueled the company's growth, while taking advantage of market timing, due to the recent political climate of racial justice awakening expanding awareness of the company's product.

Resources

- Digital Behavioral Startup Hurdle Raises $5 Million to Help Underserved Communities—Behavioral Health Business: https://

bhbusiness.com/2021/01/27/digital-behavioral-startup-hurdle-raises-5-million-to-help-underserved-communities/.

References

Bond, M. J., & Herman, A. A. (2016). Lagging life expectancy for Black men: A public health imperative. *American Journal of Public Health*, *106*(7), 1167–1169. https://doi.org/10.2105/AJPH.2016.303251

Cambridge Dictionary. (n.d.). Systemic racism. In *Cambridge Dictionary*. Retrieved from https://dictionary.cambridge.org/dictionary/english/systemic-racism

Coward, K. (2021, January 27). *Digital behavioral startup Hurdle raises $5 million to help underserved communities*. Behavioral Health Business. https://bhbusiness.com/2021/01/27/digital-behavioral-startup-hurdle-raises-5-million-to-help-underserved-communities/#:~:text=Hurdle%2C%20which%20was%20formerly%20Henry%20Health%2C%20was%20founded,The%20company%20rebranded%20itself%20as%20Hurdle%20last%20August.

Dictionary.com (n.d.). Stigma. Retrieved from https://www.dictionary.com/browse/stigma

Hargrave, M. (2022, August 5). *Capital: Definition, how it's used, structure, and types in business*. Investopedia. https://www.investopedia.com/terms/c/capital.asp#:~:text=Capital%20is%20a%20broad%20term%20that%20can%20describe,financial%20assets%20of%20a%20business%20or%20an%20individual

Investopedia Team. (2023, May 22). *Target market: Definition, purpose, examples, market segments*. Investopedia. https://www.investopedia.com/terms/t/target-market.asp

Hurdle Health. (n.d.). Startup Health. https://www.startuphealth.com/hurdle

Lindsay, D. (2022, June 15). *Hurdle Health partners with Oscar Health, Inc. to provide people of color with greater access to mental health services*. Business Wire. https://www.businesswire.com/news/home/20220615005176/en/Hurdle-Health-Partners-with-Oscar-Health-Inc.-to-Provide-People-of-Color-with-Greater-Access-to-Mental-Health-Services

Merriam-Webster. (n.d.). Synthesize. In *Merriam-Webster.com dictionary*. Retrieved from https://www.merriam-webster.com/dictionary/synthesize

O'Malley, L. (2021, November 17). *Addressing the lack of Black mental health professionals*. Insight into Diversity. https://www.insightintodiversity.com/addressing-the-lack-of-black-mental-health-professionals/#:~:text=Background,percent%20of%20psychologists%20are%20Black.

4

Bison Venture Partners

The Problem of Supporting and Funding First-Time Founders

Concept Highlight

management consulting: the practice of consulting for business challenges throughout an organization. Project teams are typically paid to provide recommendations to senior-level executives. This is also commonly a costly effort to analyze potential solutions before the organization invests resources to address issues at the firm.

investment firm: a group of investors who have pooled their resources to support smaller businesses. Sometimes, investors will play an active role in developing firm progress by providing noncapital support. Advising startups is common, which may be linked to board seats or strong influence by way of shares. Capital tables (documents) often show the breakdown of shares. These tools provide clarity for investors and inform the term sheet to follow.

financial condition: a general term used to describe the health of the organization, deriving from the cash position of the firm. For further reading see, the four financial statements, chart of accounts or profit and loss statements by business vertical—often referred to as P and L.

milestones: a colloquial term for major accomplishments within the specified period of time. The term is derived from journeymen or race traveling, where at each mile, a stone would be placed to designate the distance traveled.

short-term expenses: operational overhead that may be fixed or variable. Fixed costs may be salary commitments to full-time employees or contractors. An example of variable would be utilities that fluctuate.

Introduction

While reading this case, you may learn about startup challenges you may not have been exposed to until now. The concepts discussed in this case study will be helpful for you in your business studies. This student-led startup provides the ground floor view of how founders leverage their background toward building a team and attracting capital. This case study is included to spur your thinking about problems the business is facing in its early stage of development. By the end of this case study, you should be able to identify issues and provide suggestions on how the firm should scale.

Learning Outcomes

- Understand the founder's vision and how that directly ties to their market research as well as what they believe they can execute based on tight feedback loops with their potential customer base.
- Identify and articulate issues within a case.
- Identify risks of the business and articulate them.

Key Terms Used in This Chapter

- **Black-owned business:** a business with majority Black ownership.
- **crowdfunding:** the practice of funding a project or venture by raising many small amounts of money from a large number of people, typically through the internet.
- **founding team:** the group of people who come together to divide ownership of a business. Typically, all founders are at the executive level. Rarely, founders may not have equity in the business at all; in other instances, founders' equity may vest at a particular milestone of the business defined in time or revenue.

- **Kickstarter:** an American public benefit corporation, based in Brooklyn, New York, that maintains a global crowdfunding platform. This dynamic tool provides a venue for all levels of investors to participate in equity rounds.

Section I: Business Description

Bison Venture partner advises businesses on profitability strategies, improves investment readiness, access to capital, and builds pathways to wealth and creates sustainable community impact.

Section II: Founder History

Garry Johnson III is an award-winning startup founder and nationally recognized ecosystem builder, working to build a more inclusive and equitable innovation economy. Johnson has been recognized as a *Delaware Business Times* 40 Under 40 honoree, HBCU.vc & Hen Hatch Pitch Competition Winner, StartupAfrica Youth Entrepreneur of the Year, and Siegfried Award Recipient, among other accolades. He enjoys sharing his views as an innovation activist in op-eds, such as "Delaware Business Community, You're Officially on Notice," published in Technical.ly Delaware.

He received a BS in exercise science as well as an MS in entrepreneurship and design from the University of Delaware. While currently teaching as an adjunct entrepreneurship professor at UD, he is also pursuing an MBA at Howard University.

He's the founder and executive director of First Founders Inc., a 501(c)(3) organization on a mission to lower barriers to entry and increase the likelihood of success in the innovation ecosystem. The organization helps early stage entrepreneurs launch successful startups through accelerator programs, community support, and access to resources. The First Founders community currently includes more than 200 entrepreneurs from around the world and has helped them raise over $300,000 in nondilutive funding.

His startup experience includes launching an award-winning fintech startup that provided solutions in small business lending and personal financial management. He's passionate about supporting the Delaware startup ecosystem by serving on the Tech Forum Board of Directors and Horn Alumni Council. Nationally, his entrepreneur support experience ranges from advising teams in the National Science Foundation's I-Corps programs, mentoring startups in Backstage Capital's Philadelphia Accelerator, and supporting the launch of the BH Ventures Accelerator in Houston, Texas.

Section III: Company History

Bison Venture Partners (BVP) was founded in August of 2021, following the orientation for Howard University's MBA program. BVP has been "building in public" and launched the company to the public through a Wefunder "Testing the Waters" campaign to raise awareness and startup funds for the business. In April of 2022, BVP officially filed its Form C with the SEC, making its campaign a public offering, where it could begin accepting investments from the community. Over the last year, BVP launched an apparel brand called Black Unicorns, started an ecommerce marketplace called HBCU.market, and have begun consulting with several startups gearing up to raise their own community rounds.

Section IV: Current Challenges

Bison Venture Partners was founded by Garry Johnson III a couple weeks into being a candidate at the MBA program with fellow students. Johnson describes his motivation to enter into entrepreneurship and some initial obstacles he faced. While reading, imagine you are meeting entrepreneurs and learning about how to support them along their journey. As you go further into analyzing their businesses, think through resources they may have leveraged that are directly related to their goals. Be mindful that Johnson's journey is specific to the problems BVP addresses and your analysis should be tailored to his business:

> We want to make sure generational wealth is at the forefront of our message. One challenge is we are students who are building a business. I'm a full-time entrepreneur and my teammates are full-time employees somewhere else. One challenge is we all want to be full time and have access to capital.

We are currently fundraising from the community. That is absolutely our biggest challenge. We have a goal of raising $250,000 through a platform called Wefunder. While inviting both accredited and unaccredited investors to learn more about our work.

The beauty is we could go to our community, this is still a very new thing to do. A new way to fundraise means a new behavior. People in our community are not as familiar with this process. The most investing they might be doing is in the stock market. Educating the market is challenging to shift that behavior. We've raised over $50,000 from over 100 individuals. Our assumptions about the ease of fundraising have been a challenge. From a user experience standpoint, they are not necessarily reading everything. For the most part, the minimum is what people do when we don't meet with them while they are usually inspired when we do meet with them.

Over time, the team gets more comfortable with making the pitch. The pitch is easy, the Q&A is the harder part. The team has helped us scale the network. One of our team members is based in Texas and his network of mentors has been helpful. We are leveraging technology, making it really easy to schedule time with us, which increases the number of touches we get. Questions about the raise become booking a 15-minute time slot. They might DM questions.

TikTok has required the most investment to build that up, it could be the most powerful tool if a post would go viral. When we launched twitter, that was the best. It's a great platform for me personally. We are very much comparable on Twitter for the audience there. From there, LinkedIn is in second place—not that we've gotten many investments yet. Higher dollar investors come from there.

Community is our differentiator. We are not currently managing a fund. If we did, we would only be able to raise institutional funds and venture capital which limits us. If we simply raised the fund, that would not be the solution. Our community needs community input, investment, and investment readiness programming.

Sources and avenues of funding are critical for our community to understand. Our community may not be leveraging the most appropriate funding. We can get them set up on a campaign that is most appropriate for them and take a critical look at their books. We don't have to manage anyone's money to do that and that's a differentiator. The beauty of it is ownership all around, that's why we focus on crowdfunding (G. Johnson, personal communication, August 2021).

Company News

Take a look at the following news on Bison Venture Partners to learn more about the company vision and an additional resource to discover more about how the company messages its value proposition to the primary customers and investor base:

- Episode 31: "Garry Johnson of Bison Venture Partners"—Inside Startup Investing With Chris Lustrino: https://open.spotify.com/episode/2jF48S7YoVKV2chyfbncNS
- "How to Invest in Bison Venture Partners": https://www.youtube.com/watch?v=yOWHFfsQb5s&ab_channel=1867Studio

Key Takeaways

- Young, diverse, and Black professionals are finding entry points into venture capital through unconventional routes.
- Fundraising relies on community and the founding team is intentionally tapping into several communities to build relationships in multiple entrepreneurial ecosystems.
- Innovation requires assessing the new behavior desired and investment in educating the consumer to think differently about the established norm. In this case, crowdfunding is a shift in investing.

Resources

- Bison Venture Partners: Building a More Equitable Future for All—WeFunder: https://wefunder.com/bisonvp
- Bison Venture Partners—Crunchbase: https://www.crunchbase.com/organization/bison-venture-partners
- Bison Ventures—CB Insights: https://www.cbinsights.com/investor/bison-ventures
- Bison Ventures (Washington) Overview—PitchBook: https://pitchbook.com/profiles/investor/495629-56

- Delaware-connected firm Bison Venture Partners aims to 'disrupt the trillion dollar blind spot'—Technical.ly: https://technical.ly/diversity-equity-inclusion/garry-johnson-equity-crowdfunding/
- Bison Ventures Management Co LLC—Bloomberg: https://www.bloomberg.com/profile/company/2040999D:US
- Bison Venture Partners—Lustro: https://crowdlustro.com/search/4913-Bison-Venture-Partners-on-Wefunder
- "Delaware Business Community, You're Officially on Notice"—Technical.ly: https://technical.ly/diversity-equity-inclusion/garry-johnson-delaware-business-community-youre-officially-on-notice-racial-equity-black-founders-entrepreneurs-access-resources-funding/

5

TipSnaps

The Problem of Creator Payments Where FinTech Meets Crowd Marketing

Company News

Read the following article on TipSnaps's fundraising campaign results for more context on the company, how they structure their campaign and articulate their solution for creators, and how they consider their market size. Specifically, as you perform this cursory browse, think through what other sources of information might be helpful to look through before diving deeper into this case: "PPV Crowdfunding for Social Media Content in the Creator Economy" (https://republic.com/tipsnaps).

Concept Highlight

- **contractor support:** hired expertise that works on defined hours, is part time, has their own equipment, and performs duties defined by a scope of work that details what they are accountable for in their contract.
- **development road map:** a plan that dictates when and how feature updates will occur during the course of development. When startups raise funds, it can be critical for the technical team to understand their development/product roadmap to meet market demand. This plan impacts expenses, due to the manpower needed for programming and coding.

- **fintech:** short for "financial technology." Tools and solutions developed and labeled as fintech often reduce friction for consumer payments.
- **influencer marketing:** a form of social media marketing that leverages endorsements on products and services from an expert. While reading this case, you should examine this concept and understand how TipSnaps creator payments diverge from this concept.

Introduction

While reading this case, you may learn about startup challenges you may not have been exposed to until now. The concepts discussed in this case study will be helpful for you in your business studies. Grappling with the leadership decisions and organizational strategy will help you gain sophistication for pending challenges in your career. This case explains the founder's decisions and encourages you to read between the lines on what's not included in our brief company description. The macroeconomic factors that inform the founders' vision to develop their product–market fit is of great importance for you to consider. Zooming out in this way will help you understand the case and help inform how you approach your analysis as well as your recommendations.

Learning Outcomes

- Understand the founder's vision and how that directly ties to their market research.
- Learn to detail what they believe they can execute based on tight feedback loops with a potential customer base.
- Identify and articulate issues within a case.
- Identify and articulate risks of the business.

Key Terms Used in This Chapter

- **active users:** those who regularly engage in a product experience, often measured
- **angel investor:** $5,000–$100,000 investments from individual investors who may or may not identify as accredited investors. These actors may commit to and participate in syndicate funds or communities of investors.
- **audience engagement:** when the target community is actively in communication with the company via newsletters, text alerts, promotions, advertisements, experiences, posts, stories, video, and/or calls
- **point of sale:** when and where a product or service is purchased
- **product–market fit:** when the product being developed has a business model that the target market has embraced. To scale into secondary and tertiary markets, the product can be adapted on pricing and features to meet these needs. Initially, product fit to market speaks to the buyer exchanging money for the seller's product. For more information, review minimum viability products and what constitutes a market.

Section I: Business Description

TipSnaps enables anyone with an audience to monetize it directly, giving power to creators (TipSnaps, n.d.a).

Section II: Founder History

Lyonel Douge, the chief executive officer of TipSnaps, studied computer engineering at the University of Pittsburgh. He worked in corporate for more than a decade before starting TipSnaps. He started the company in his after-work hours and was able to raise $200k from an angel investor, Pat Condon, at Active Capital (Huddleston, 2022).

Vic Boddie is the cofounder and chief operating officer of TipSnaps. Dr. Boddie is an experienced regulatory affairs team lead with a track record of excellence, leading an award-winning compliance program at the U.S. Food and Drug Administration. Vic has an established history of leadership in regulatory affairs at the FDA. During his 9+ years at the FDA, he's led numerous cross-functional compliance program areas, such as unapproved drug regulatory policy initiatives, strategic policy initiatives for oncology products, COVID-19 regulatory policy, and the development of drug compounding policy (GFI-256). Vic leads these ongoing efforts to protect public health while serving as a direct advisor to FDA senior executive leadership (V. Boddie, personal interview, April 2023).

Section III: Company History

TipsSnaps was founded by in 2017. Its CEO, Douge, worked for Sony and Viacom with angel investments beginning in 2020. Their initial prototype created revenue within a week, which proved the concept for further development to generate 60,000 creators within 2 years (Huddleston, 2022). The business supports personal brand monetization, without leveraging ad revenue or paid product endorsements (TipSnaps, n.d.b). The platform uses a subscription model for one-time payments and recurring monthly access.

Creators retain ownership published on the platform, which and charges a commission of 15% per subscription at point of sale or tip on their managed content that is labeled “high-risk.” The difference between TipSnaps and other platforms that prioritize content is there is no shadow banning of Black creators, as seen on other platforms, and TipSnaps actively teaches creator entrepreneurship. TipSnaps also plans to enhance tax filings for its creators.

Section IV: Current Challenges

The current challenges of the business were captured in an interview with the founders. Early stage businesses tend to face challenges attracting and sustaining stage-appropriate talent. As the company grows, many firms desire to bring talent with them to activate institutional memory. However, not all team members are inclined to stay or are the best fit to stay for the company's next stage of traction.

Additionally, TipSnaps is very clear on their values of having a diverse founding team and diversity in community with their customers. These core values have influenced how they look at their growing business. The following quotes come from my conversations with the founding team, and I have the honor of sharing them with you (V. Boddie, personal interview, April 2023):

- "We have gone through the gauntlet of entrepreneurship. As an engineer and technical person, the thing was as a unique product developed; we could win. A lot of our counterparts were much more about user acquisition through social media presence and developing relationships with investors prior to having anything built. That seemed to be more important than anything else. For personality types like mine, it was more about the build for me," says Douge.
- "Being true to who you are has been our thing," says Douge.
- "One of the later challenges with a working company, it's critical to understand your customer and where they are. It's one thing to build a product but can't underestimate the marketing and the selling of the product. A lot of the viral successes of the past 5 years are potently connected to the consumer. Our advice is don't divorce yourself from your consumer. Always seek them out. Understanding where they are and truly developing the relationship. The flywheel should come together and take care of itself. Early on look for growth hacks," says Douge.
- "We want to make sure we are where the target consumers are. Literally, on IG, where they are, not where they are not," says Douge.
- "Relationships are key. Even if you have done everything above, you should meet people with the intent of learning something from them. Not in a transactional sense. Friendships and advocates come from genuine interactions. It is ineffective to meet people simply when you need something," says Dr. Boddie.
- "Launching in 2017, as one of the creator economy products we bootstrapped to $600k in revenue and 100k users. If I was better networked then, I would have gotten a seed investment then, but I worked in corporate for many years. I went the traditional route of college and had a decade of experience. Meanwhile, all the innovation was happening elsewhere, outside of corporate. If I could go back and do it again, I would have worked for a startup and gotten exposure to that ecosystem. I started to develop relationships.

As a Black male founder, we get about 2–10x the resistance of our counterparts," says Douge.

- "When we first pitched it, we got that resistance and response that this is influencer marketing. We said, no it's not that. Then our White counterparts pitched a similar thing with less expertise and traditional money doesn't trust us," says Douge.
- "When 98% of venture capital is going to white founders, we could have gotten a white face to go to bat for it. We are good enough to have the life experiences that execute this work. Including, processing payments, including growth hacking and having the team to get it done. We build relationships with people and follow up. I don't have any issue with the black founder going that route, but that's not our path," says Douge.
- "One of the things "that has enabled us to grow is that the world is small due to technology. There's still a lot of untapped potential based on the resources we have. We've hired offshore resources in the Philippines for $5 an hour for our English as a first language. We know we would prefer stateside resources as part of our internal operations. It would be great to come back to our hometowns as well to build (Virginia, etc.). We also want our company to be representative of who we are. We want to hire black and brown engineers, lawyers, HBCU graduates, young people, and Gen Z. We are not going to build this company and then have it look like DEI issues of other companies. There is no DEI issue here. We will show and prove this [as] we have for years [and years]. We want our executive board to also look like the communities we serve as well. That will happen too," says Dr. Boddie.

Key Takeaways

- Team development at early stage ventures can be contractor rich, meaning bootstrap and early raise budgeting may restrict full-time employment status and abundant compensation above market rate. Contractors with strict scopes of work are pivotal for early team development. Full-time employees are often costly on taxes and benefits, which may look like reduced value and be against the values of an organization but may also be a business imperative.

- Equitable compensation in financial technology can be baked into the business model.

Resources

- TipSnaps—Republic: https://republic.com/tipsnaps
- TipSnaps—KingsCrowd: https://kingscrowd.com/tipsnaps-on-republic-2022/
- TipSnaps Overview—PitchBook: https://pitchbook.com/profiles/company/469569-25
- TipSnaps—LinkedIn: https://www.linkedin.com/company/tipsnaps/
- Black-Owned social media platform with 450k users announces equity crowdfunding campaign on Republic—PR Newswire: https://www.prnewswire.com/news-releases/black-owned-social-media-platform-with-450k-users-announces-equity-crowdfunding-campaign-on-republic-301507833.html
- Tipsnaps Information—RocketReach: https://rocketreach.co/tipsnaps-profile_b437913dc1fcf350
- TipSnaps—Tracxn: https://tracxn.com/d/companies/tipsnaps.com

References

Huddleston, T. (2022, March 4). *This 37-year-old launched a social media company with 400,000 users—while keeping his day job.* Make It. https://www.cnbc.com/2022/03/04/he-founded-tipsnaps-while-still-working-his-full-time-day-job.html

TipSnaps (n.d.a). Crunchbase. Retrieved from https://www.crunchbase.com/organization/tipsnaps

TipSnaps (n.d.b). Everybody Wiki. Retrieved from https://en.everybodywiki.com/TipSnaps

6

CarpeDM

The Problem of Engaging a Billion Dollar Customer Segment a Niche Product Expansion

Concept Highlight

- **channel partner:** an organization in the same market, serving as a conduit for an ask. Channel partners are typically engaged with to achieve traction in the target market via referral, advocacy, or amplifying the value proposition of another business. A channel partner could create an agreement simply for marketing and promotions or for many other purposes. These include, but are not limited to, a contract to purchase services at bulk and subsidize early adopters.
- **promotions:** creating marketing assets to draw the target audience into a funnel for the business and then engaging the audience at specific times of day and in an intentional sequence
- **mission and vision alignment:** the connection between the desired impact of an organization and the predicted outcomes aspired to by the imagination of the founding leader(s)
- **fractional C-Suite:** similar to a contractor at lower levels of the organization. These executives may engage 2 or 3 days a week in their role. This role is best performed by high-performing leaders with considerable experience at more than one company, as they are required to and responsible for being efficient. Compensation is often hourly, by retainer, or by monthly fees.

Introduction

This case is included to think critically about lifestyle technology. The company has been selected for you to consider how these type of businesses have reduced friction for consumers with every day applications. Consider strategic implications of convenience in our society and how this affects product development. These considerations will help you gain sophistication for pending challenges in your career as well. Again, not simply the takeaways but the analytical exercise involved in answering how and why we solve lifestyle challenges with technology.

Learning Outcomes

- Learn how technology development has its challenges and opportunities.
- Understand that community building is about experience development as much as it is about product development.
- Measure the strength of these experiences and pursuing deeper understanding of frictions in the early stages of the business evolution.

Key Terms

- **channel partners:** organizations and individuals that connect to the company's desired audience for customers.
- **membership strategy:** the member experience anchors the community developed for the firm. An engagement strategy anchors the process of ensuring the touchpoints for each participant is consistent with the brand and appropriately manages expectations.

Section I: Business Description

CarpeDM Dating is an exclusive online dating community designed primarily to engage Black women. Matchmaking services and a customized algorithm were engineered to produce better dating outcomes for this premier community. The company has deployed this niche dating app with rapid plans for expansion, due to their verification of daters through background checks, questionnaires, video interviews for men, rewards and giveaways for experiences, and events. The company has created a social club on and offline, following the model of Black professional chapter-based communities throughout the country. Their founders are HBCU law grads, with both negotiation and marketing skills in the forefront.

Section II: Founder History

Naza Shelley is the founder and CEO of CarpeDM. She is a lawyer by profession, having graduated from Howard University School of Law in 2011.

Sali Hama is the cofounder and chief marketing officer at CarpeDM. She graduated from Howard Law the same year as Naza. They went on to pursue senior-level legal work in public service and corporate law. For close to a decade before pursuing their first tech venture, they built skills in the workplace that now inform their team-building strategy, workplace culture, and growth strategy.

Section III: Company History

CarpeDM was founded in 2018, and its first iteration, a video-first dating app, following a freemium model, launched in 2019. The MVP product was released on iOS and Android, and the company gained over 10,000 users before pivoting during COVID to a niche subscription-model service targeting an underserved and under-leveraged segment of the dating industry: professional Black women.

The company won the 2020 Technica.ly Invention of the Year award, due to its solution to the dating challenge for Black women; in 2021, CarpeDM won Technical.ly Startup of the year; and in 2023, CarpeDM won the *Washington Business Journal* Startup Madness competition, besting 15 other local startups. Cofounders Naza Shelley and Sali Hama were law school classmates who researched data on the value of relationships that provide economic, physical, and mental support that led them to take action. The team created an interactive virtual dating show, called

LoveCast, to shine the spotlight on the growing community of singles in the DMV area. They followed the dating show with an app in 2022. The company focuses on the holistic experience for daters, including background checks, social verification, insights on dating better with emotional intelligence coaching, and events. Creating a culture of community and strategic partnerships for marketing amongst six different organizations in their primary target market followed their first launch.

Section IV: Current Challenges

CarpeDM's founders shared the following current challenges to capture the top-of-mind issues facing the company:

- "For many startups, raising the capital needed to grow your business is a central challenge. This is true for the CarpeDM team. To date, they have raised over $1.5m in institutional capital, joining the less than 1% of Black female owned, and women led businesses to raise from VC."
- "I am grateful for the problems I have today, because these are the problems I was asking for last year."
- "Accelerator commitments and decisions. CarpeDM participated in the Conscious Venture Labs Accelerator and Techstars. The return on investment for these are a concern when our product and business growth is high priority. Community building is imperative in our work, and we need to be present in the variety of ecosystems where we aim to gain traction and raise money. Often in that order, or those two goals run parallel."
- "Hiring key staff while we grow membership creates a challenge we are currently facing. The chief financial officer and marketing manager would allow me to do more decisions on the business, instead of in the business. Our fractional chief operating officer will also be a decision to help accomplish the aforementioned."

Company News

Public relations have been increasingly pivotal for CarpeDM. As user acquisition is critical to growth for this venture. The firm has been featured on national television and produces a regular cadence on their blog as well as social media. The founding team strategy also includes a chief marketing officer to tell the story of the value proposition and member experience across audiences. Read the following news story on CarpeDM as well as the company's mission statement:

- "Virtual Dating During Social Distancing"—Fox 5, Washington DC: https://www.fox5dc.com/video/670261
- "Carpe Diem's Mission Statement": https://carpedmdating.com/#mission

Key Takeaways

Business success includes community development. In the dual-sided marketplace, matching is predicated upon value on both sides to meet the expectations of each customer. In this way, supply must meet demand. If not, imbalance can undermine the value proposition.

- Traction for these founders has a specific definition that can be understood by satisfaction metrics:
    - launched waitlist and received over 3,000 applications
    - fully launched service in December 2022, beating Q1 23 revenue metrics by 20%
    - grew team from 3 to 12 in 1 year
    - raised additional VC capital for bridge round in 2023
    - features in *Essence*, *Black Enterprise*, *Blavity*, *Washington Business Journal*, and *Washintonian*
- Acceleration of growth may also mean shifts in the team. The roles and duties of the founding team have shifted as the needs of the business shift with maturity of the venture.

Resources

- KarmaCheck Partners with CarpeDM, an Exclusive Online Dating App for Black Women Pioneering 100% Member Background Checks—PR Newswire: https://www.prnewswire.com/news-releases/karmacheck-partners-with-carpedm-an-exclusive-online-dating-app-for-black-women-pioneering-100-member-background-checks-301441204.html
- CarpeDM is launching its dating app for Black women this fall—Technical.ly: https://technical.ly/startups/carpedm-dating-app/
- D.C.-area founders and funders make their predictions for the startup scene in 2021—The Business Journals: https://www.bizjournals.com/washington/news/2020/12/30/predictions-for-the-dc-area-startup-scene.html
- Virtual Dating Shows Are Popping Up To Play Matchmaker For Local Quarantined Singles—DCist: https://dcist.com/story/20/04/17/virtual-dating-shows-are-popping-up-to-play-matchmaker-for-local-quarantined-singles/
- Everything that happened in LoveCast episode one—NBC Sports Washington: https://www.nbcsports.com/washington/other-sports/everything-happened-lovecast-episode-one
- Is Love Canceled Too? Dating At A Distance During Coronavirus—The Kojo Nnamdi Show: https://thekojonnamdishow.org/shows/2020-05-05/is-love-canceled-too-dating-at-a-distance-during-coronavirus

7

NURILENS

The Problem of Finding Culturally Inspired Eyewear

"Get to know your business and not compare it to everybody else's pace."

"We understand our competition, but my brand has a story and it's ok that I get stuck here and there. I don't cave into every single temptation. My business plan has been my anchor to continue learning and move forward."

"Generation X is very loyal. They keep coming back to us. We now focus on improving that through surveys and iterating on the experience consistently."

—Dr. Juliette Nelson

Concept Highlight

- **strategic public relations:** marketing strategy that attracts mentions of the solution offered by the startup and positions the founding team in a positive light where customers and partners are high in traffic.
- **operational clarity**: day-to-day execution of the businesses aligned with the vision of the firm and its strategic plan. Absent a strategic plan, operational clarity often aligns with customer feedback and market demand.
- **founder–market fit:** an indicator of a match between the founder and the industry they are attempting to enter. This likely includes specific

achievements in their professional experience and relationship capital in their personal network.

Introduction

This business was included to bring your attention to a niche solution in a growing marketplace of unique goods. Read this case while thinking through how differentiation can be valuable to consumers and investors alike. In other words, how being different can be a significant advantage while also limiting the mass distribution of a product. Read for what this does for your vision in specializing in an area of your career, evaluating investment opportunities as a future investor, or assisting a venture with a narrow solution. The concepts below should push your thinking as you read through the founder's inspiration and product vision to serve a population of curious and conscious consumers.

Learning Outcomes

- Understand founder vision and how that directly ties to their market research.
- Identify and articulate issues within a case.
- Identify risks of the business and articulate risk-management strategies.

Key Terms

- **audience engagement:** the target community being in active communication with the company via newsletters, text alerts, promotions, advertisements, experiences, posts, stories, video, and/or calls
- **brand clarity:** image, firm reputation, and delivery of core competencies are understood both internally and externally among stakeholders

- **investor risk:** the assumed downside of capital investment defined by both qualitative and quantitative measurement
- **origin story:** the beginning of the problem–solution fit and founder journey, which may include some deeper inspiration and quantitative insights that lead to deeper time and energy investment in a startup journey
- **point of sale:** when and where a product or service is purchased
- **product–market fit:** when the product being developed has a business model the target market has embraced. To scale into secondary and tertiary markets, the product can be adapted on pricing and features to meet these needs. Initially, product fit to market speaks to the buyer exchanging money for the seller's product. For more information, review minimum viability products and what constitutes a market.

Section I: Business Description

NURILENS is an eyewear company that offers afrocentric frames and lenses for customers. The company specializes in handcrafted wooden frames. They engage diverse audiences that encourage self-expression and sustainability. The frames can be purchased with the upgrades often seen at easy-to-purchase eyewear companies, like Warby Parker and LensCrafters. According to the NURILENS homepage, available features include anti-blue light lenses, high-index lenses, superhydrophobic lenses, and installment plans.

Section II: Founder History

Dr. Juliette Nelson is an industrial–organizational psychology professional, educator, and entrepreneur passionate about encouraging people to live their lives with meaning and purpose. She founded NURILENS out of her desire to express herself through her love for fashionable eyewear as well as a need for affordable vision solutions. Having traveled to different countries and lived in South Korea for a year, she was exposed to a variety of fashionable and inexpensive eyewear options that allowed her to express her colorful personality and individuality. Reflecting on her journey to celebrating her identity and history and living out her purpose, NURILENS is a means by which she encourages others to do the same. It seeks to combine style, performance, and sustainability by creating an experience that encourages self-expression, impact, and improved eye health.

Section III: Company History

Dr. Nelson (J. Nelson, personal interview, February 2022) tells us a bit about her path to startups:

> In 2012, I made the crazy decision to fly halfway across the world, and work in South Korea for a year. I was exhausted from my high school and college journey. Also, unlike my peers, I didn't have any job offers lined up when I graduated, so I needed an escape. It was something that I wasn't even sure I'd do until the plane was flying over Japan and I realized that it couldn't turn around. That year was the beginning of the definition of Juliette. It was my first time living outside my parents' house. I learned so much about who I was, and what I accepted as my truth. It was there that I discovered my passion for empowering and uplifting others.
>
> During my last few days in South Korea, my pastor, who was also the director of my school, gave me the Korean name, Na Nuri. It comes from the Korean verb, Nanuda (나누다), meaning "to share." He commissioned me to share my gift wherever I would go. I remember asking God to use me to touch people from different backgrounds and cultures. I didn't know what that meant, but those words were profound and would set a precedent for how I would ultimately grow.
>
> South Korea was not only the place I found my purpose, but also where the seeds for NURILENS were planted. Since childhood, I have loved to collect everything; keychains, cheap watches, brooches, and other things that allowed me to express my personality. Glasses were no different. Living in South Korea, I realized that I could get several affordable pairs of eyewear that were fashionable and would match my different wardrobes. So, I started stacking up. I think at some point, I must have purchased about 20 pairs. Some had bling, others had swirls, and were of different shapes and sizes. Interestingly enough, when I founded my first company, JUNURI, in 2018, I remember saying that the next pair of glasses I purchased, would

be ones that I have personally designed, but I never took myself seriously. Ironically, the same glasses that I had for years, started breaking within months of my founding NURILENS.

In 2019, I discovered the world of blue-light blocking glasses, that gamers often wear to reduce the eye strain from playing video games all day. I saw the benefits and became interested in learning more. Given that my primary clientele for JUNURI was students and professionals, it caused me to think how they too, sit for hours in front of their screens, and would benefit from this. As someone who also sits for hours in front of a screen every day, I would also benefit from them. Months later, I worked with optical professionals, who helped me understand how to fill prescriptions, for people like me who need corrective lenses. I then put pencil to paper and sketched out designs for glasses, which led to me to buy my first sketchbook. Letting my creativity flow on paper felt great and liberating. (NuriLens, n.d.)

Section IV: Current Challenges

The current challenges of this business are connected to the retail goals for the firm:

- "Pop-up events have shown transactions, but the goal is to do better with trimming costs. Lens manufacturing challenges and brand awareness for new products."
- "Generation X and the tail end of baby boomers. They have the most influence on millennials, baby boomers, and beyond."
- "We're in the process of doing 2.5 rebrand of the product to improve the look and feel of the brand without stripping the essence of the brand. That's what customers connect with a lot. Because it's a personalized product, customers want to interact with the staff."
- "We have been collecting qualitative data to take note of what questions customers are asking. We include that in our product development process, to measure what they look at first and improve the customer journey."
- "We have an optometry tech who leverages research on eye health and is aiming to bring more wellness approaches to eyewear. We

have started to put out content to make this connection. We bring awareness through *The Visionary* podcast."

- "Lens supplier is in China and their holiday calendar is a challenge for us because they all shut down during that time. Trying to find the sweet spot between supply and demand with our suppliers. There may not be enough revenue coming in to cover those costs of fulfilling orders. We prefer to have a U.S. manufacturer and have started selling accessories to keep customers in our funnel (i.e., lens cleaner and wood polish)."

Company News

This venture has produced some copy to engage their customer base on identity and belonging. Core to the company's mission is to elevate voice of their customers and prospective customers, while carving out a lane for diversity in eyewear that has limited traction without them. The following resource is included for your exploration:

- *VisioNURI* Podcast: https://www.buzzsprout.com/2006079

Key Takeaways

Building an eyewear company has unique challenges that this firm has managed to overcome. The early journey of brand clarity and telling the story of the founder resonates highly with the target audience. The look and feel of the product is consistent with the origin story and has had a lasting impact on how the company sustains itself. Customers always want customization; however, how this is executed, how to appropriately price it, and how to scale it depends on many variables. The difficulty can be overcome with adequate customer research and testing.

Resources

- NURILENS: https://nurilens.co/

- Why NURILENS Is The Haitian-American Luxury Eyewear Line You Need To Know—Yahoo! News: https://news.yahoo.com/why-nurilens-haitian-american-luxury-163848161.html?guccounter=1&guce_referrer=aHR0cHM6Ly93d3cuYm-luZy5jb20v&guce_referrer_sig=AQAAAJKAQxP4uPYNgUD-KzG_4Kd-Cump5eNW-YJmzMncyuvyk0J6lWMYOQ0yL-VqZhWs5TpRHIp6slmHbGbU3mt0pc7umTyiK1FgZYQMXA32eEr-pw-WCW2WepK99lRqac9xQDrjq-4Uf-91NHcIWbCBTZLe0MF67h_M2pv_7tiHKs88RCH
- NURILENS—Black-Owned Association: https://blackownedas-sociation.com/listing/nurilens/
- Black-owned eyewear brand NURILENS advocates for better vision care—AFRO News: https://afro.com/black-owned-eyewear-brand-nurilens-advocates-for-better-vision-care/
- NURILENS—Haitian Businesses Directory: haitian-businesses.com/fashion/nurilens
- The Haitian Luxury Eyewear Line You Need To Know—Black Wall St Media: https://blackwallst.media/the-haitian-luxury-eyewear-line-you-need-to-know/
- NURILENS—Virginia Black Business Directory: https://members.vablackbusinessdirectory.org/directory/Details/nurilens-1716104

Reference

NURILENS. (n.d.). Our Story. https://nurilens.co/pages/our-story

www.ingramcontent.com/pod-product-compliance
Ingram Content Group UK Ltd.
Pitfield, Milton Keynes, MK11 3LW, UK
UKHW020138250726
13967UKWH00002B/721

9 781793 574787